FAMILY WORK:

WHOSE JOB IS IT?

WRITTEN BY LYNN LOTT,

RIKI INTNER, AND MARILYN KIENTZ

A BOOK FOR HARRIED HOUSEWIVES, FRUSTRATED
FATHERS, AND COMPLAINING KIDS

Copyright 1988

Published by The Practical Press
P.O. Box 2615
Petaluma, California 94953

Printed in the United States of America

Second Printing September 1989

The Practical Press

Family Work: Whose Job Is It?

Library of Congress Card Number 88-060627

ISBN 1-882023-00-5

$9.95

Dedicated to our children, Casey & Corey, Samantha,
David & Jennifer, and Philipa, Richie, Aaron & Marcie
with our wishes for a more cooperative tomorrow.

TABLE OF CONTENTS

INTRODUCTION

This book is about families working together. It's never too late to start. All we need to know is HOW to do it and WHY bother. We cover both the HOW and the WHY in this book. The HOW is broken down by age in Chapters 3, 4, and 5 and by specific examples in the "Question and Answer" section at the end of the book. The WHY is explained in the Introduction and is woven throughout the book. (If you picked up this book and started reading it, you probably already have your own answer.

As family educators and family therapists, we work with many families who have benefited from the suggestions in this book. Our own families have also become closer and more capable and cooperative from following the steps we've outlined. We've discovered a formula that illustrates the WHY. It goes like this:

Useful, capable, skilled people tend to handle life's tasks and problems successfully.

When work is handled by agreement instead of assumption, families run smoother, feel closer, and are happier.

Add these two together and you have families working together, liking being together, and pulling together.

We live in a complex, challenging time. In every house there's an opportunity for family closeness, participation, shared decision making and skill development. Some of these can be accomplished through play, church or community activities, but they can all be done within the family through Family Work. Any group of people who live together have things that need to get done. Working together can provide a sense of belonging, contribution and camaraderie. As parents we have the opportunity to increase our influence with our children and help them be more capable by showing them how to be interdependent through Family Work.

This will require some effort and involve some change. But it may prevent more serious problems from cropping up in our homes later on. Research shows that people who feel capable, needed, and interdependent tend not to abuse drugs, disobey the law, abuse their children, or give up.

Whether you're looking for changes in the present or you're concerned about the future, this book can show you how to set up Family Work and make things better for everyone in your home--whether there are two of you or ten.

CHAPTER 1 - WORKING TOGETHER

For many of us, the WHY of setting up family work begins with a picture that looks something like this:

Welcome! You've just entered the home of the typical family in Anywhere, U.S.A. Look around. There are toys, shoes and magazines on the floor and piles of clean laundry on the sofa waiting to be folded. There's dirty laundry waiting next to the washing machine to be washed. Dinner needs to be started, but the counters are cluttered and someone tracked mud all over the kitchen floor, so making your way to the kitchen sink is in itself an adventure.

If you looked in the other rooms you'd see that the

bathrooms need to be cleaned and the trash baskets need to be emptied. If you took the trash outside, you'd notice that the garbage cans are full, the lawn needs mowing, and the leaves on the shrubs are beginning to curl from lack of water.

This house is full of what we call Family Work. It doesn't really matter if the family who lives here is a traditional family of Mom, Dad and 2.3 children where the inside cleaning jobs are left for Mom and the yard jobs are left for Dad, or if this is a picture of a single parent household where Dad will come home to three children and begin dealing with the mess, both inside and outside the house. In some cases it might even be a kid who thinks he or she is responsible for getting the work done. The important point to remember is that there is usually one person in the family who thinks it's his or her job to take care of everything--inside or outside--the house, even though he or she may feel tired and resentful. This person has often decided that it's less of a hassle just to do things rather than argue or nag.

HOW DID THIS HAPPEN?

As unbelievable as it may sound, these families, like so many in our society, has been trained to function this way. Society gives us messages, and one particularly powerful message is that men and women have separate and definite roles to fulfill: men are the "breadwinners" and women are the "homemakers". Women take care of the "inside" of the house; men take care of the "outside" of the house--and the car. Although this is changing somewhat, many women still feel that taking care of home and hearth is their responsibility--their job. They're reluctant to involve their spouses or, if they do attempt to change things, they often find themselves in arguments. Many men believe that if they work outside the home and earn a living, that's enough work for the family. Unfortunately, they continue to believe this even when their wives also work outside the home.

Single Moms and Dads are finding that the combined job of breadwinner and homemaker is both physically and emotionally draining. These parents are discovering that the old messages about men's work and women's work haven't prepared them to deal effectively with the day-to-day work of family life.

In traditional families the message that taking care of the inside of the house is Mom's job has been communicated in subtle ways to our kids. For instance, when young children want to be involved and ask to help, mothers send them outside so they'll be out of the way while Mom gets the job done. Messages that repairs, yardwork and car maintenance are Dad's job have been communicated too. Fathers also send children away when they want to be involved in his chores. In both cases we've neither trained or prepared our daughters and sons to help in all areas of Family Work.

No wonder so many parents reach a point where they feel angry and resentful. After all, being on 24 hours a day, seven days a week, is draining. We ask how we got to be responsible for it all. One of the hardest parts of changing this is that it's easy to feel alone and stuck and to think we're the only one feeling resentful. We forget or don't realize that there is another way.

There is another way, of course. We think it's by far the best way. We call it Family Work--everyone pitching in and doing his or her share. The basic premise of Family Work is that helping with things around the house is everybody's job, not just one person's job. That means Dad, Mom, little kids, big kids and everyone in between is involved. We believe that when Family Work is shared by everyone, the whole family benefits and everyone feels better.

In traditional families, fathers may worry when they hear about Family Work that the change will place an extra burden on them. They may wonder if, in addition to working fulltime, they'll have to do all of the housework too. Mothers may feel great about having help with housework but worry about giving up their control over the way things are done. For some children the idea of Family Work may be a real jolt at first.

Sharing Family Work is beneficial for everyone. When our families are more involved, everyone can experience the benefits. Mothers and single fathers can stop feeling resentful and angry for being stuck with "inside" work," and fathers and single mothers can stop feeling resentful about having to be stuck with "outside" work. We can take pride in learning to use a variety of skills. Whether we're working mothers, househusbands, single parents, or husbands and wives, we can take on new roles in the family. We become leaders, coaches, organizers, teachers, and planners, instead of maids, custodians or groundskeepers for our families. We're still needed, but in new ways. We feel better about ourselves and have a greater sense of freedom. We have more time to enjoy the things we like to do and to enjoy the other members of our family.

Fathers in traditional families can participate more fully in household management. They can gain greater closeness and a sense of belonging and importance. These new roles also help parents contribute to their children's developing a sense of responsibility and independence. Our children can feel capable, useful, important, and needed. They'll learn the importance and enjoyment of working together. Our families will become more creative, cooperative, and united.

WHAT DO WE MEAN BY WORK?

Before we get into the specifics of how to start, let's clear up a couple of things. When we talk about Family Work in this book, we're referring to those things that benefit the entire family and the chores that need to be done as part of the daily routine of family living. Cleaning one's own room or doing homework or filing one's nails would not fall under our definition of Family Work. Giving the dog a bath, doing dishes, buying groceries, cooking dinner, putting gas and oil in the car, mowing or watering the lawn and folding clothes are chores that benefit the family and that help maintain the normal routine of family living. We're not suggesting that the other tasks aren't important. But in encouraging the family to work together, it's important to emphasize the jobs that help the whole family as a unit.

AGREEMENTS INSTEAD OF ASSUMPTIONS

Family Work is work by agreement and not by assumption. We make a mistake when job division is by assumption. When we assume who will do a job. It doesn't matter whether the assumption is our own ("I think I should do this") or about others ("I think you should do this"). The key to cooperation is to change the division of jobs from assumption to agreement. Instead of expecting the kids to do dishes because they're kids, or husbands to empty garbage because they're men, or wives to cook because they're women, or parents to shop for groceries because they're adults, NOW we can say there is work to be done and we need to agree on who will do it. Instead of "Who messed up the house?", we can say, "The house is a mess, and it needs to be cleaned."

We may be in a partnership where we agree that cleaning out the refrigerator will be Mom's job or that taking the trash cans to the curb will be Dad's job. If we've discussed it and decided that's how we want to distribute that part of our Family Work then we have an agreement. If we assume that cleaning out the refrigerator is a woman's job and hauling the trash cans out on Sunday night is a man's, then we have an assumption.

Consider how we might be cheating ourselves and other family members out of a sense of accomplishment or skills by not being more involved in areas that traditionally belong to the OTHER sex--male or female!

The difference between agreements and assumption may not seem so huge--but, as you'll see, it's significant.

CHAPTER 2 -- GETTING STARTED

It's never too early or too late to get the family involved in working together. The important thing is to help our kids learn that they are important, useful, contributing members of the family. When we start late we may have to work through some bad habits. But we can still see that doing work builds skills, develops a sense of usefulness, and teaches appreciation for the work that needs to be done and for those who do it.

In the beginning it will take longer to get things done, and a lot of time may need to be spent in training. If the family has been used to having one parent do all the inside work and another doing all the outside work, or one person doing it all, they may not react to changes enthusiastically. At first the kids might think it's fun to help out, but they may soon tire of helping and want to go back to having special maid, janitorial or cooking service. Our partners may feel trapped and worried. They may think, "If I start helping with one thing, there may be no end to the demands to do more."

People who have spent years or lifetimes in families where chores were divided by sex and by assumption may find it difficult to let go of that old training. Many women feel guilty when they ask for help or don't do all of the work inside the home themselves. In spite of their resentment, many women don't feel comfortable when they step out of their traditional domestic role. They don't have a model or picture of how to include their partner without feeling guilty. Women are often afraid to give up the power that comes with managing their homes. They haven't learned how to include someone else in the day-to-day management. At the same time some men feel that their role of provider is being undermined when they work inside the house or their wives work outside the home. Both men and women may need to learn skills to do work traditionally done by their partner.

Making changes in general can be difficult and require commitment and concentration. Changing the family work pattern is one of the biggest and most significant changes a family can make. If we think that we can get things squared away in a week or so, or if we expect that when people agree to do certain tasks they'll automatically remember without any slips or reminding, we're setting ourselves up for disappointment and possible failure. It's easy to become discouraged and want to give up and go back into the old ways of doing things.

On the other hand, if we have a plan and hold on to our goals of shared responsibility, mutual respect, and work by agreement instead of assumption, the transition will be easier. It may progress by taking one step backwards and two steps forward, but it will be well worth the effort. In one of our families, which had been very traditional, the transition took about five years. Family members still slip back into their old behaviors occasionally, but it doesn't last for long.

WHAT IS THE BASIC GOAL OF FAMILY WORK?

We'd like to answer the question by sharing a picture of an actual family that has benefited from Family Work and really learned how to do it on a cooperative basis. We would have been grateful for such a picture ourselves when we started moving from being traditional homemakers/career women, who thought we should do it all, to moms and wives who learned to let go, share, teach, include, and be more open to what needs to be done.

In the morning the kids get up, clean their rooms, get ready for school, and make their lunches. Mom makes breakfast, and she and the kids eat together. Dad has to leave early, so he handles his own morning routine. After school the kids come home and do a few chores while their parents are at work. At dinner time everyone takes turns cooking, doing dishes, feeding the pets, and sweeping the floor. The person who cooks plans the menu for that meal.

Menu planning is done as a family on Sunday evenings directly on a calendar that hangs in the kitchen. From the menu, Mom makes a grocery list. Then the whole family sits at the table and, while one person reads off the items, the others call out which ones they'll pick up at the store and write them on a list of their own. Everyone piles into the car, drives to the store, grabs a cart and takes off in four different directions. About twenty minutes later, they meet at the checkout counter, done. Then it's home, where they all help unload the car, put away the groceries, and fold the bags.

On laundry day Mom does all the wash except Dad's, which he prefers to do himself. The kids fold the clothes and everyone helps put them away. On weekends they work in the yard together dividing up the mowing, trimming, fertilizing, and other chores. We don't mean to present a picture of one big happy family whistling while they work. Most of them hate at least one of their daily chores, but they love to eat, wear clean clothes and have a home and yard, so they grumble and groan and do the jobs.

As good as the final picture looks, it was accomplished through tears, tantrums, sit-down strikes, reminding, talking, and trying again, and again and again. The members of this family were social pioneers in this area and it got a lot worse before it got better. So hang on to your goals, because it's a bumpy road, with great rewards at the end.

YOUR FAMILY AT FAMILY WORK

Any people who live together have certain things that need to be done. You may be in a partnership where you agree that some chores will still be done according to traditional sex roles--the woman does the laundry and the man changes the oil in the car. If you and your partner agree that's how you want to arrange your Family Work then by all means do so. If you want to send the laundry out because no one wants to do it or you hire a mechanic to change the oil, then you have those options too.

POINTERS FOR GETTING STARTED

Read the whole book first.

You may be tempted to read just the chapters that involve children in your family's age group. We recommend reading the whole book first, as there are many ideas in each section that you may find useful, no matter what age your kids are. Reading the whole book may save you many steps in the long run.

Have a plan.

Decide on one thing to work on and how you'll proceed. Otherwise, you may tend to overwhelm yourself by trying too much at once and get nowhere. We need to retrain ourselves as well as our families. This requires focus and concentration. It's usually a good idea to live with the plan for a week before changing it, throwing it out, or adding other projects.

An example of having a plan might be to work on toy pickup. The plan could be to have a time of day when the toys need to be put away neatly and when all other activities stop until that one chore gets done. You may decide to sit on the floor with the kids during this time, working when they work and stopping when they stop. This routine could be done every day before dinner for ten minutes for one week. Perhaps the second week the cleanup routine could remain the same, except the kids could do it by themselves. Having a plan like this and sticking to it eliminates nagging, reminding, a lack of follow through, and setting up for failure. Making the plan can be a joint effort involving both parents. If one parent decides to make a change alone, the other parent should be informed and involved as much as possible.

Parents teach, not the kids.

If you have several kids, it's often tempting to ask one of them to show a younger child how to do a job or to supervise work activity and make sure it gets done. We don't recommend this. The skills and patience needed when working with a new learner are more likely to be found in an adult. Also, children get frustrated when younger brothers and sisters won't cooperate. Fearful they'll get in trouble, the older ones may tend to be bossy and punitive. Another reason for doing it yourself is that the time we spend in teaching our kids is rewarding. We get to learn more about them, how they think, and what motivates them, and they enjoy the time and attention we give.

It's not necessary for Mom to do all the training. In fact, fathers can often be more effective teaching new patterns if they don't have a history of nagging and fighting with the kids over the job. In many cases, fathers tend to talk less and act more, so the kids follow through better. Training is time consuming, and sharing the load between parents can be supportive and helpful.

Don't "baby" the youngest.

We tend to underestimate the abilities of our youngest children and keep them helpless and out of Family Work "until they're older". Also, older kids, wanting to show us how good they are by being helpful, may do too much for younger ones instead of letting them do things for themselves. Sometimes older ones do things to prevent the younger kids from helping, like criticizing, jumping in, and doing the job first or doing it over. But kids need a chance to be involved in Family Work. There's plenty to go around, and it's a great way to feel a sense of belonging, usefulness, and success. So make sure you don't keep someone out because of age. Instead, go out of your way to think of things they can succeed at and do to help.

Act without talking.

The single most important change we can make to improve cooperation at home is to talk less and act more. If we say things over and over or give long explanations or lectures, we're talking too much. If we're trying to motivate our kids with words or yelling, it probably won't be effective.

Let's say that one of our kids has agreed to do a job and hasn't done it. Instead of yelling from another room, we would be more effective by getting up, going to where the child is, standing where we have eye contact, and saying once, "You need to empty the garbage" (or whatever). The rest is up to the kid--we don't have to argue or explain. All we do is stand quietly and wait. Try it! The results can be amazing.

Another way of acting instead of talking can be to lead a younger child by the hand to a task rather than shouting directions from another room. Sometimes we can act persuasively by omission--for instance, if the dirty clothes aren't in the laundry, we can decide to wash only the ones that are there and not chase down kids or clothes. If toys aren't being picked up, we might decide to put them in a box on a shelf and leave them there until the weekend. The important point is to SAY IT ONCE and then ACT.

Action is more likely to happen if we're standing up, so another suggestion is not to say anything unless you intend to follow through and when you speak, STAND. That way, if any action is needed, you're already halfway there.

CHAPTER 3 - INFANTS TO FIVE-YEARS-OLD AND BEGINNING WORKERS OF ANY AGE

Here are some tips that will make the job of getting the family working together easier and some ideas for starting with children who are between infancy and five years old. If your children are older, the tips in this section can be helpful in insuring success, especially if the idea of Family Work is new in your house.

1. FOCUS ON PROGRESS, NOT PERFECTION.

2. WATCH YOUR LANGUAGE AND CHANGE YOUR MESSAGES.

3. RETRAIN YOURSELF: THINK "WE", NOT "I".

4. LEARN TO LOVE A LUMPY BED.

5. MAKE IT EASIER. USE JOB CHARTS, SCHEDULES, AND OTHER VISUAL AIDS.

6. USE LIMITED CHOICES.

1. FOCUS ON PROGRESS, NOT PERFECTION

When your two-year-old "helps" you set the table and the silver ware is upside down, or when your three-year-old wants to push the vacuum and the room suddenly seems ten times bigger, it's easy to say, "Here, I'll do that. You go out and play." If you do that instead of focusing on progress, not perfection, you'll miss a chance to get the family involved.

17

How do you go about focusing on progress? Try the following:

Do Family Work when the kids are around so they can help instead of saving it until they're napping or at school. This takes some advance planning.

Teach on the fly. If you're cooking and your child says, "Can I help?" say "Yes!" and demonstrate how to crack an egg or stir the soup.

Emphasize the fun of work and make it a game whenever possible. Have a race putting the toys away, or race a timer, or throw things into the toybox from a few feet away.

Avoid power struggles by not making an issue out of finishing the job or doing it your way. Be glad the kids are involved and let them know their help is appreciated.

Take one step at a time. This is important with younger kids and those who are new to working with the family. If getting the kids helping with dishes is a goal, one step would be to help them learn how to clear the table or scrape a plate. Even though it may be tempting to teach the entire process all at once, it's less overwhelming if kids can learn step by step. Focusing on a manageable piece of the job is very encouraging for new workers.

Set up a training time to help your children (or your spouse) learn how to do the job. Don't assume they know how. When they feel they know how to do the job, or when you think they're ready, pull back, but let them know you're available if they need you.

Work with the kids. Have a "work time" when everyone is doing a job, even if each job is different. The idea is for everyone to work at the same time together.

Take instant pictures of the kids standing next to a finished job. Start a scrapbook or stick the pictures up on the refrigerator or bulletin board.

2. WATCH YOUR LANGUAGE AND CHANGE YOUR MESSAGES

The way we teach beginning workers sets the stage for the future. It's important to consider how the things we say can affect the direction we're heading. What messages would we be giving our children with the following statements?

PARENTS SAY THIS:	OR	PARENTS SAY THIS:
1. Let me do it!		You try!
2. Go out and play.		Here's a feather duster so you can help.
3. You're too little.		Want to swish the brush in the toilet?
4. That's not the way. Let me finish. Let me redo that.		Thank you. I'm glad you like to help.
5. Here, I'll do that.		What would happen if you tugged a little harder on the corner?
6. I have to do this before the kids get up.		Cleanup time. Let's work together.
7. Let me get this work done so we can play and have fun.		Let's do this together so it'll go faster and we'll have more time at the park.

20

The messages kids might hear sound like this:

1. You're not capable.   You're able to do things.

2. Parents work; kids get to play.   Work can be enjoyable.

3. You're incompetent.   You're capable.

4. You don't do things right.   Your help is appreciated.

5. You don't need to learn.   You're able to figure things out.

6. Kids get in the way.   Everyone can contribute.

7. Work isn't fun.   We can help each other work and play together.

3. RETRAIN YOURSELF: THINK OF "WE", NOT "I"

The early years are a good time to train the whole family to get involved. Establishing routines stimulates cooperation and avoids power conflicts. Kids relate well to order and structure. But getting family members working together requires advance planning and the belief that you really don't have to do it all!

If you think ahead you can plan so you share the work. You can stimulate cooperation and get a chance to teach on the fly. For example, to clear the table, make a line of family members from table to sink and play "pass it along." When it's time to put toys away, work with the kids. Ask, "Where does this go?" while handing the child a toy to put away.

Work as long as the kids do. When they stop, you stop.

To get your spouse involved, ask him or her for help. Work together on a new project that you've never done before.

Have special times for doing jobs with enforceable deadlines. Some examples are:

Before breakfast, the kids should have their rooms cleaned, clothes and shoes on, and beds made. If it's not done, place their breakfast plates upside down on the table as a nonverbal reminder--they can return to the table as soon as the work is done.

Before dinner, have a family straightening time (pick up around the house).

During Saturday morning shopping, the kids can help

you by finding a can of peaches or a box of cereal.

Before bedtime on Sunday, water the plants.

On laundry day fold towels or carry clean clothes to the children's room .

Make the kids their own cleaning kits: feather duster, small broom, cleanser, and so on (for outdoors it might be a small shovel and a short rake), so they can work with you. Thank them for what they do. Don't complain when they leave, get tired or cranky.

On special occasions--for example, when company is coming--instead of sending the kids outside, find jobs that they can do. Some ideas would be making personalized place cards, putting candy and nuts in bowls, making table decorations, and dusting.

The focus is on setting a pattern so that work is part of life and a daily routine. Gradually the family learns that Family Work can be fun as well as challenging and everyone is needed to get it all done.

4. LEARN TO LOVE A LUMPY BED.

If you're constantly redoing your child's work or correcting them, it won't take long before the kids decide to stop helping. Kids hear what we do more than what we say. If we say we want their help but then redo everything, they'll know we really don't mean it. This applies to our mates, too. It can be a real challenge for the meticulous housekeeper, and it may mean letting go of having the house exactly the way you want it or "perfect."

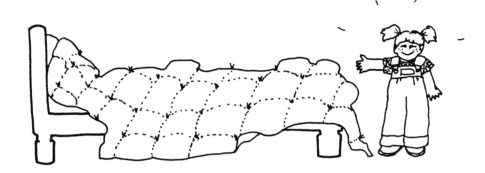

Once when a daughter of one of the authors was three, she helped prepare for company by cleaning the toilet (her choice). After the company left at the end of the evening, Mom went into the bathroom for the first time all evening. To her dismay, she noticed her daughter had used the entire can of cleanser and the bathroom was filled with the stuff. Their gracious guests had used the bathroom many times during the evening and never said a word.

You might not believe it, but you can learn to enjoy a "clean" bedroom where the bed is made but full of lumps and the floor is clean although the toys are under the bed. If the kids did it themselves and are proud of their work, the lumps won't look so bad.

When your kids start a new job, it's important to take time for training, but after training you should pull back unless needed or invited. For many of us, that will be a big challenge. It helps to keep our long term goals in mind.

5. MAKE IT EASIER: USE JOB CHARTS, SCHEDULES AND OTHER VISUAL AIDS.

For young children charts can be amusing, nonverbal reminders that will help them remember routines. When it's work time, the chart can speak instead of a nagging parent. For instance, Mom or Dad can say, "Would someone look at the chart and see whose turn it is to feed the dog." By showing each person's part, a chart also demonstrates vividly that everyone is part of the whole effort. Job charts should be simple and contain pictures. If the kids can help make them, all the better.

Having a time of day when the job charts are checked, the jobs are done, and everyone works together is another effective strategy. Right before or after dinner is a natural for this. Include everyone in the house on the job chart. Let the kids help name jobs that EVERYONE could do. Rotate jobs daily or weekly at this age, and take time to train the family on the "how to's" of the job.

This chart is an example of one that can be used for a family of four. The chart is made on a paper plate with magazine cutouts for pictures and a brad in the center so the chart can be rotated daily. The chart shows jobs that can be done before dinner.

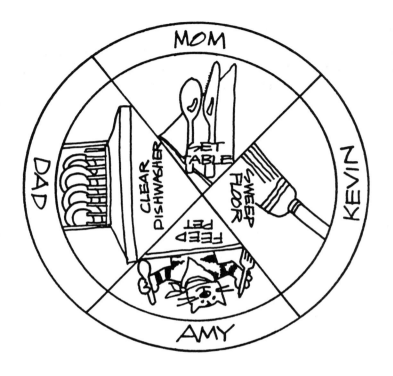

6. USE LIMITED CHOICES

It is especially important with very young children to avoid turning work into a power struggle. Unfortunately, this is an easy trap to fall into. How often have you heard a mother say, "Johnny, pick your truck up. NOW!" only to get, "No, I won't" for a reply? When we command or demand that our children do things according to OUR time schedule or precisely the way we'd do it ourselves, we set the stage for a conflict. Also, when we ask questions like "Do you want to pick up your truck?" we're just as likely to get "No" for an answer.

By using limited choices with our children, we can define the limits while providing freedom of choice within them. It's a good way to win our children's cooperation in getting the job done. If we say, "Johnny, do you want to pick up your truck or your ball first?", we're letting Johnny know we expect the job will be done. But we're also communicating that he has some choice in what he wants to begin with. It's important to keep these limited choices simple and to the point. Here are some examples:

"Do you want to dust the table or the bookshelves?"

"Do you want to put the silver out or the plates?"

"Do you want to put your toy on the top shelf or the bottom shelf?"

Once the limited choice is given, it doesn't need to be repeated. After the words comes the time for action. If a child gives an unacceptable third alternative to a limited choice, it's OK to say, "I'm sorry, that's not one of the choices."

CHAPTER 4 - "FAMILY WORK" FOR CHILDREN FROM SIX TO TEN-YEARS-OLD AND THE FAMILY THAT IS WORKING TOGETHER

All the steps from the previous chapter are still important as the kids get older or the family becomes more comfortable working together. But now we can add some additional points to consider.

1. FOCUS ON ONE THING AT A TIME.

2. INVOLVE THE KIDS IN PLANNING CHORES.

3. ACT AND FOLLOW THROUGH.

4. RESPECT THEIR STANDARDS.

5. WATCH OUT FOR PINK AND BLUE RIBBONS.

6. ADD MORE JOBS AND MORE RESPONSIBILITY.

7. REDIRECT YOUR EFFORTS--BECOME A CONSULTANT AND CO-WORKER.

8. SET UP EXTRA JOBS FOR PAY.

1. FOCUS ON ONE THING AT A TIME.

Don't try to accomplish too much at once--that way, you'll risk everything. Instead, think about a small task that you would be willing to work on for a week. For instance, maybe you'd like to help the kids get in the habit of getting dressed themselves before school. Focusing on only that for one week is a large enough task. Once you know what you want to work on, you can sit down with the kids and discuss a possible routine with them. Suggest choices like: "Do you want to lay out your clothes the night before or pick them out in the morning?"; "Would you like me to call you when breakfast is ready, or shall we set a timer?"; "If you come to the table undressed, would you like me to turn your plate upside down as a reminder to go finish or should I just tell you?" After setting up the task with the kids, the rest of the week can be spent in follow through and practice. This means the parent acts without talking, reminding, and nagging.

A single parent was having trouble getting his kids and himself off to work on time. He was spending most of the morning coaxing and nagging, but still everyone was late. He decided to set up a routine with the kids, get them alarm clocks, and stop talking. He told the kids they would have to leave with him at 8:00 a.m. no matter what state they were in. After three or four mornings of chaos, tears, and half-dressed kids piling into the car without breakfast, the kids learned to plan ahead and get ready. As a result, Dad is more relaxed and the day goes better for everyone.

Another way to think about having a plan is to decide which task we will share with the kids or at which time of day we will make an effort to involve the kids in work. Again, the idea is progress, not perfection, and retraining yourself is a big part of getting off to a good start with family work.

2. INVOLVE THE KIDS IN PLANNING CHORES.

Often Family Work fails because one member of the family tells everyone what to do instead of asking for their ideas. A simple process for involving the family is:

A. Invite everyone to sit down together and let them know you need their help.

B. Ask what work needs to be done for the family to function smoothly. Write down all ideas even if they seem silly. Don't worry about ideas that might have been missed. This is a start, not the final solution.

C. Ask if each person would be willing to pick one to three things to do for one week.

D. Decide when the job needs to be done, how often it needs to be done, and when it needs to be finished. Write that down too.

E. Post the list.

F. Whoever normally did the job before the family planning meeting can show the new person how to do it. That person also continues to do any job that hasn't been chosen. Remember, the idea is to settle for progress, not perfection.

Don't worry about getting all the jobs divided up. Overwhelming everyone with tasks would make it difficult to win cooperation. This is just for one week. Changes can be made and other jobs can be added later on. Whatever comes of the first week, it's bound to be a lot better than doing everything yourself.

Another way to distribute jobs is to list them, write them on separate pieces of paper, throw the pieces in a hat, and have each person pick one to three jobs for the week.

If the family has the habit of thinking one person should do it all, a good approach is to appeal to the family's sense of fairness and ask, "Who thinks it's fair for one person to do all the work? Who wants to? I certainly don't and I'd like us to work together."

3. ACT AND FOLLOW THROUGH.

Once the jobs are set up, distributed, and posted, it's best to let a week go by and see what happens without nagging, reminding, or interfering. This is often difficult for families to do, but it takes time to learn a new habit. You might make problems you don't need in this transition period if you begin reminding the kids to do their jobs because you expect them to forget them. Chances are the kids will forget, almost because it's expected. Wait and see if a problem gets to be a pattern, rather than overreacting the first time someone forgets.

At the end of a week, the family can sit down together and review their progress. If jobs haven't gotten done, it may be time to move to Phase Two--setting up a consequence if work doesn't get done. Consequences need to be **related, respectful,** and **reasonable** in order to work. Some possibilities are:

Live with the job undone. For instance, garbage not emptied piles up, rooms not picked up look awful, an unmowed lawn gets longer. This isn't forever, just until the end of the week, when everyone in the family can learn from the experience if nothing is said.

Set up a work time when everyone works together.

Set a deadline. For instance, jobs not done before dinner must be completed before people eat. Work first, then food.

Set up an "inconvenient reminder" system that everyone agrees on in advance. For example, jobs forgotten and not done as agreed must be done as soon as a reminder is given, no matter how inconvenient the time--like in the middle of a favorite TV show or a few minutes after getting into bed.

Decide what you will do, such as refusing to cook in a messy kitchen. In some families, the parents may chose to eat out until the kitchen gets cleaned, even if it's only at an affordable fast-food restaurant. The parents' attitude must remain friendly, firm and kind, or these options can turn into the beginning of a giant power struggle or revenge cycle.

Jobs undone get done by someone else for pay and the person who didn't do his or her job pays either in service or in money.

In another family each child has a tag with the list of jobs that need to be done. Before dinner the children check their tags. When the job is completed, they turn the tag over to their picture, which is on the other side, and they can come to dinner. If their job isn't complete yet, they do it before coming to the table.

4. RESPECT THEIR STANDARDS.

Too often problems arise around shared involvement in Family Work because one person sets the standards for the outcome. Yet one person's idea of "clean," "organized," or "straightened" may not be the same as another's. Another person's way of doing a job often leads to creative new ideas and a sense of "our home" instead of "Mom's home" or "Dad's home."

In one family a mother came home one day to find that "her" kitchen had been reorganized. At first she was angry because the changes made it hard for her to function, but soon she realized that this drastic measure accomplished two important things. First, the kids were able to reach and find things more easily. Second, the ownership of the kitchen had changed from "Mom's" to "the family's."

In another family, letting the kids help with the shopping resulted in the addition of some new cleaning products that worked better than the old ones. The kids had seen one of their friend's mom using the new product and wanted to try it out when they did their own cleaning.

When someone else does a job, a new perspective is introduced. In one family, the grocery shopping was done by the mom and the kids. Dividing the list was done at the store and proved to be difficult and bothersome. When Dad got involved, he suggested the family divide the list at home, where everyone could sit at the table with a paper and pencil and write their items down. Not only did this work better, but it became a game with everyone shouting out the items they most wanted to shop for.

5. WATCH OUT FOR PINK AND BLUE RIBBONS!

If our goal is to raise responsible kids who do things because they need to be done and because it will benefit the whole family, it's important not to stereotype jobs by sex. Boys can cook, do dishes, and fold clothes, and girls can wash cars, mow lawns, and empty garbage. Moms can learn to change the oil and Dads can cook dinner. Instead of "men's work" and "women's work," there's just "work that needs to be done."

Making these changes is not always easy. When one mother overheard her child ask Dad to go shopping for shoes, she felt sad and worried that she had been replaced and the kids wouldn't need her anymore. In another family, the mother decided it was time to take more responsibility for her own car. She had watched her husband change the oil and thought it looked pretty easy to do. She started the project and accidentally tightened the oil filter instead of loosening it. Three hours later the job was finished, with the help of AAA. The next time the oil needed to be changed, she responsibly asked her spouse to show her how, and he made himself available to assist her as she learned to do it.

Changes may not come easily, but the following example illustrates how effective your teachings about Family Work can be.

A boy we know had dinner at a friend's house and came home in shock when he noticed that the mom cooked the dinner, set the table, served the food, waited on the family, and then did all the cleanup herself. His comment was, "Can you believe that there are still some families where the mom does all the housework and the rest of the family lets her!"

6. ADD MORE JOBS AND RESPONSIBILITY.

As your kids get older they can do more and harder tasks. Perhaps they started out helping the family work before dinner by emptying the dishwasher. Then later they added a job after dinner, too, like clearing the table. Now they could add some chores before breakfast, such as cleaning their rooms and making their lunch for school or helping one day a week with the major house cleaning or yard work.

In one family when the kids got involved in weekly cleaning, they started out with a chart. Since their mom had done most of the cleaning up to that point, she decided that breaking down each room into simple do-able tasks on a chart would be a good way to begin training the rest of the family. The family started out with each person cleaning two rooms of the house and everyone working at the same time. The mom was available to show them how and to assist them for several weeks, until the kids and their dad felt competent to do the task without her help. The family decided to pay themselves for the work they did by putting the money saved by not hiring someone into a jar and using it for family fun outings. This system of shared work has lasted them throughout the years. What used to be drudgery for one has become a chore for many that gets done in less than one hour a week.

One family took a similar chart and put it on the kitchen table each day. Each family member went off and completed a job, came back and marked it off, went off to do another, and so on. Weekly cleaning was finished when all the jobs were done, and then the family spent time together doing a fun activity such as a picnic, a trip to the park, or playing a game.

Another family wrote all the jobs to be done on slips of paper and put them in a bag. Included on the slips of paper were some items like "Go outside and sing a funny song" or "Rest for five minutes." Each family member did the job as the assignment was pulled out of the bag, including the "fun" things.

Adding more responsibility can work in another way. For instance, making a lunch for school may start off with something as simple as the child making a peanut butter sandwich. Later on it can progress to putting the entire lunch together. The next step could be having the kids shop for their own ingredients or even having a lunch budget so they can plan what they want to buy at the store or at school. Later still, the focus might change to planning lunches that are more nutritious or varied.

7. REDIRECT YOUR EFFORTS -- BECOME A CONSULTANT AND CO-WORKER.

When your kids were younger or newer to working, they needed more direction from you. As they gain more work experience, you can work along with them. It's fun to ask your kids if you can assist them and let them give you directions. You can pull back and be nearby if needed, but you don't have to be right in the middle of things.

It helps to ask the kids if they want your input or ideas before automatically giving it. For instance, saying, "I have an idea about how you might get the sink cleaner. Are you interested in hearing my idea or would you like to figure it out by yourself?" might be more appropriate at this age than just telling the kids to do the sink over or accepting a poor job.

It's also important--and fun--to get kids of this age more involved in planning and cooking meals. At first they might suggest a meal a week and assist the cook. Next, they could cook it themselves, with the parent assisting them. After that, they can choose the meal, cook it, and have one parent nearby if needed for help. Finally, they'll be able to cook even if the parent isn't home. This kind of responsibility building can be exciting both for parents and kids. If the kids have friends over, their friends want to get in on the action and cook too.

One family meets on Sundays so that everyone can sign up for her or his night to cook the following week. The kids love rotating the cooking because they're guaranteed that at least one night a week they'll be eating something they love. Also, on the nights they cook, their parents pitch in and take a turn at doing the dishes. The kids sign up for one night a week, Dad signs up for two, and Mom does two or three nights unless the family goes out. This arrangement has resulted in the family eating a variety of new dishes that they'd never tried before. Everyone now has a particular specialty dish, too, like Dad's Stir Fry, Sis's Barbeque Ribs, Bro's Fettucini, and Mom's Vegetarian Delights.

8. SET UP EXTRA JOBS FOR PAY.

Perhaps you've noticed we haven't suggested paying family members to do jobs. We believe that work is a tool for teaching kids responsibility, skills, cooperation, and the importance of being a contributing member of the family. Work needs to be done so the family can function. It should be kept separate from allowances. We do suggest paying the kids for jobs that we would hire someone else to do however. For instance, one of us was taking the car to the local carwash and spending $2 each time. When our kids asked for ways to make extra money, we told them we'd be happy to spend the same amount of money and hire them to do the job. We suggest keeping a list of paying jobs on a bulletin board with the amounts to be paid for each job so anyone who wants to earn extra money can do so if he or she wants.

In some families the jobs shown on our "Jobs for Pay" list might be considered routine, and then the parents wouldn't pay to have them done. Remember, a good rule of thumb is to ask yourself whether you would hire someone outside the family to do the job. If so, the job could be for extra pay instead of part of the normal routine of Family Work.

Jobs for Pay

Washing Windows = 50¢ window

Cleaning Cupboards = 25¢ cupboard

Shelling nuts = $1⁰⁰/½ hour

Polishing Silver = 25¢ a place setting

Stacking Wood = 50¢ single stack

We recommend that allowances be given to kids regularly-- they're family members, and they should have the opportunity to learn about having and using money responsibly. The amount can vary with the age of the kids, their expenses, and the financial circumstances of the parents. The time to start allowances is when your kids begin to have expenses--gumballs at the grocery store. Many a parent has made the trip to the store more enjoyable for everyone by starting an allowance and reminding the kids to use it when they start making demands at the store.

CHAPTER 5 - FAMILY WORK FOR KIDS ELEVEN AND OLDER
NEW OR RELUCTANT AND EXPERIENCED WORKERS

Children eleven-years-old and older may have two very different experiences with Family Work. One possibility is that they haven't been involved in helping much, either because it wasn't expected or it didn't work. The second is that they've been very involved and have a good deal of experience with Family Work.

If you're dealing with the first group, new or reluctant workers, we recommend that you review the sections in this book on working with younger children. The same principles can apply to older kids with a few changes. In addition to those pointers, we add a few new ones.

NEW OR RELUCTANT WORKERS:

1. UNDERSTAND THE TANTRUM OF THE "PAMPERED FAMILY."

2. BE SENSITIVE TO THE FEELINGS OF THE UNTRAINED KID.

3. LEARN TO USE NATURAL AND LOGICAL CONSEQUENCES.

4. DON'T MAKE QUALITY AN ISSUE.

5. HAVE A SENSE OF HUMOR.

If you're addressing the second group, experienced workers, then these pointers apply.

EXPERIENCED WORKERS:

6. LOOSEN THE REINS FOR EXPERIENCED WORKERS.

7. WHEN THINGS STOP WORKING MAKE A CHANGE.

8. WATCH OUT FOR PITY TRAPS.

9. BE CREATIVE IN ADDING NEW WORK EXPERIENCES.

10. ENCOURAGE WORK OUTSIDE THE HOME.

11. FOCUS ON KEEPING AGREEMENTS AND THE MEANING OF "FAMILY."

1. UNDERSTAND THE TANTRUM OF A "PAMPERED FAMILY."

Use your own imagination for a moment and pretend you live in a home with a full staff of servants. They cook for you, clean for you, entertain you, and spend most of their energy making your life as pleasant as possible. All of a sudden, for no apparent reason, they all quit. They inform you that they'll do some things, but from now on, you'll be expected to pitch in and start helping out. Can you imagine jumping up and down with glee saying, "Oh thank you, thank you for not doing everything for me anymore!"? Instead, you'd probably be shocked, disbelieving, angry, scared, and determined to get them back in your service. Or at least hire new servants.

This fantasy may be what it's like for your kids if you've done everything for them, or for your mate if you've been "in service."

Let's look at what happened in a family where a teenage daughter assumed the role of housekeeper for her two younger brothers and single father. The girl decided she could no longer be in everyone's service. The father didn't really want the daughter to assume all the work, but he would be at work or the kids would be involved in activities away from the house. The household management verged on chaos. The father didn't know how to deal with all the "housework," and the daughter did. Her brothers gave her a hard time, saying she was being unfair because all their friends' moms made their lunches, did the cleaning, and didn't expect the kids to work. "After all," they said, "we're just kids and kids are supposed to have fun." One of the brothers thought it would be fun to help out, but not all the time.

At first the daughter felt guilty and frustrated about the mess and went back to her old ways, even though she was very resentful. However, both she and her father soon realized that the family was having a kind of temper tantrum associated with change. They decided it was understandable and okay for the family to be angry, just as it was okay for the daughter to want housework to be shared. The father was then able to move forward with firmness and kindness instead of anger at the family's behavior. Once it was clear to the family that Sis was not going to be the maid and that there was no going back, they could then decide what they wanted. This family decided to begin with absolute basics like meeting once a week to make work more equitable and shared.

2. BE SENSITIVE TO THE FEELINGS OF THE UNTRAINED KID.

In almost all cases when we can't do something, it's not because we're inferior, but because we're untrained. For some reason, that's hard for many people to admit, and it's even harder for the kids.

One boy we know had his friend over for dinner. The friend was 14 and a bright, capable kid. When it came time to clean up, he disappeared. The next time he came for dinner, he pulled the same disappearing act. The kids in the family went to get him to help out, and he went through every excuse in the book about why he couldn't. What they finally discovered is that he had never done a dish in his life and just plain didn't know how. At his age this was embarrassing to admit, so his ploy was avoidance. The kids made a game out of teaching him how to do dishes, and a half hour later he produced the shiniest broiler pan in the family's history.

We need to let our kids know it's all right not to know something and it's okay to ask for help and to learn.

3. LEARN TO USE NATURAL AND LOGICAL CONSEQUENCES

Most of us talk too much. When our kids don't follow through, we remind, scold, nag, lecture, and generally rattle on. For our kids words go in one ear and out the other. Sometimes they listen and get angry and then use work as a way to get back at us. This can be accomplished by doing a job poorly or doing a job only when asked or later than agreed.

If you're feeling frustrated about work left undone or poorly done, it may be time for consequences. One type of consequence is a natural consequence. What would happen if you did nothing? For instance, let's say one of the kids agreed to set the table and "forgot." You could serve all the food, call the family to the table, and sit down even though it wasn't set. If you said nothing, probably the "forgetful" child would suddenly remember about agreeing to set the table. If one of the kids has agreed to cook and forgets, you could read a book or watch TV as if nothing were wrong. Probably as it got later someone would get hungry, and wonder about dinner. The key is to DO and SAY nothing and allow the "forgetful" child and the family to experience the consequences of their behavior. Natural consequences are most effective with older kids who might use chores as a battleground for fighting with their parents.

Sometimes a "logical consequence" makes more sense. Let's say someone has agreed to mow the lawn and "forgets." You may not want to do anything. You could just watch the lawn turn to hay. That would be a natural consequence. But a "logical consequence" might be more useful. You can say to the kids, "Not cutting the lawn when you've agreed to is not a choice. I'm unwilling to nag and remind. Therefore, we need to think of a consequence that happens when you 'forget' that will help you remember to cut the lawn as agreed. The consequence needs to be **RELATED,**

45

REASONABLE, and **RESPECTFUL**. Do you have any ideas? Let's brainstorm." Some   possibilities would be . . .

-- The lawn has to be cut before dinner--no dinner until the lawn is cut.

-- Work comes before play--TV and friends have to wait for the lawn.

-- If the lawn is "forgotten," an inconvenient reminder to cut it during a favorite TV show may be needed.

-- Someone else can be hired to cut the lawn, and the money to pay that person comes out of the child's funds.

It's important to find a choice everyone can live with and then try it out for one week or an agreed upon amount of time.

Here is an example of a logical consequence one family used. The kids agreed to clean their rooms once a week. If the room wasn't done before Sunday morning, they agreed not to go anywhere or do anything until it was done. One Sunday morning some friends came by and asked one of the kids to go bike riding. He asked his folks if he could go and they said, "Remember our agreement?" He had to tell his friends he couldn't ride because he had work to do first. He was grumpy and sullen, but he did what he'd agreed to do. His parents knew the consequence in itself was enough and refrained from saying things like "Maybe next time you'll plan ahead!" or "Stop acting so grumpy; it's your fault."

4. DON'T MAKE QUALITY AN ISSUE.

Often at this age, parents expect more from their kids and

criticize jobs not done according to their standards. Focusing on the effort and help may be more important than complaining about things that are done sloppily or forgotten. If a job is really done poorly or only half done, you can ask the child to come back and look around and see if they feel satisfied with their work. You can also say, "Try again, I think you can do better" or "The job isn't done. Please finish it." You can also talk about and agree on standards beforehand.

5. HAVE A SENSE OF HUMOR.

Older kids enjoy a sense of humor and respond to it much better than lectures and nagging.

In one family when the kids forgot to set the table, Mom ladled the stew onto the table one evening. The shock and absurdity of the situation had everyone laughing. Afterwards the table was set on time.

In another example, when Mom was getting too serious during menu planning, one of the kids started to do an imitation of her. Mom was always trying to get the kids to save money by planning meals from ingredients around the house, so when he imitated her he walked over the jars of staples and said, "Now we have a lot of popcorn and rice left, so Dad, why don't you make a rice and popcorn casserole?" Mom got the point and everyone had a good laugh.

One parent used betting and guessing games to motivate the kids and lighten up the situation. He'd say, "Someone forgot to do something they agreed to, and I'll give a dollar to the first person who guesses what it is." Another time he said, "I'll bet two dollars that you can't finish your yardwork before the football game starts." When these bets and games are infrequent and unexpected, they can be a lot of fun. They're very different from a reward system, where bribes and money are the only motivation for work.

Once at the grocery store, one parent took the shopping list, tore it in half and gave half to his son and his friend saying, "A dollar to each of you if you can find everything on your half of the list in fifteen minutes. Go!" Shoppers watched in surprise as the teenagers ran through the store throwing items into their cart.

6. LOOSEN THE REINS FOR EXPERIENCED WORKERS.

There comes a time in families when everyone has been working together for a long time, and we trust that the kids know what needs to be done and will do it without our interference. They may want to try new ways to do things or new timelines. They may lose interest in some jobs or change their own priorities. At this age, the kids may even want their parents to let them decide completely if, how, and when their rooms are to be handled.

When kids are younger, it's not a good idea to let them keep their rooms any way they like. Doing that may lead to so much chaos that the kids will get overwhelmed and not know where to start. It may also create problems if the kids don't learn how to organize their rooms. Parents can be important teachers at this age. Once children are older and know how to organize, they may choose not to. At this time it's important for the parent to let go and loosen the reins, allowing the kids the choice of how they want their rooms kept. If they choose to live in chaos, this doesn't mean we have to suffer as parents. We can leave clean laundry outside the door, and we can turn the task of doing their own laundry over to them. Focusing on keeping the common areas clean but letting kids be in charge of their own rooms may be difficult for the parent, but it is very positive for the kids who want a bit of the universe they can control. If we can't stand the way the room is kept, we can always close the door. When we can give kids a little space, they feel more like working with us in other areas.

Sometimes the kids will come up with a totally new plan for getting things done. In one family, one of the kids volunteered to mow the lawn every week if he could be guaranteed he wouldn't have to do any other yardwork. The family said they would try it out for a month to see if the new plan would work and reevaluate at that time. By the end of the month, everyone was pleased with the way things worked and noticed that there was much less hassling over yardwork.

When the kids have friends over, they might not get things done on the regular schedule. Unless it becomes a problem, try to go along with it, trusting that the kids will remember and do what needs to be done once their friends leave. If it gets to be a problem, you can have an agreement that either the work gets done before friends arrive or it gets done while the friends wait or pitch in and help.

7. WHEN THINGS STOP WORKING--MAKE A CHANGE.

Often one parent has more at stake in an equitable distribution of work than other members of the family and puts a lot of time and energy into motivating the family, teaching others, and training. In the beginning there may be resistance, but soon the rest of the family pitches in and is more involved. They may actually enjoy helping out. Maybe they feel it's inevitable, so why fight it? There may be periods, however, when the family gets sluggish or falls back into their old patterns and little if anything that the family needs to do gets done.

When this happens, it's time to make a change. Sitting down with the family and talking about what's going on is a good start. Maybe the family needs a vacation from Family Work. Maybe it's time to change jobs. Maybe someone has gotten into nagging and needs to stop. In one family the result of a breakdown of cooperation was a major change in the work distribution and schedule, including more casual dinners for the summer, with everyone fending for themselves instead of the usual sit-down family dinners.

At times like this we need to hold onto our picture of equality. We also need to remember that our families do want to work together and will, once the kinks get ironed out and the issues behind the slowdown are brought to the surface.

8. WATCH OUT FOR PITY TRAPS.

As parents we often feel protective of our children. We want them to have a variety of experiences, to enjoy themselves, to be happy. When our children get older they become more involved with their friends and have more social commitments. Schoolwork and homework also may become more demanding, and there may be more of it. When our children say, "Do I have to do the dishes tonight? I have so much homework I'll never get it all done!" or "I'll do the lawn next week. All the kids are going to the movies and I don't want to miss out," it might be easy to feel sorry for them and begin to take over their jobs.

But when we start to pity our children and take on their responsibilities, we're disrespectful. In doing this we aren't granting them the maturity to handle their obligations, and we're not taking care of ourselves. Sooner or later we start to feel over burdened and resentful.

When these developments occur, instead of feeling sorry for our children and taking on their jobs, it may be time to talk about rescheduling Family Work or set up a family meeting to redistribute tasks. Be flexible--but don't let your older kids off the hook. They're part of the family too.

The following example illustrates another way you might be tempted to feel sorry for your kids. In one family Mom had been helping the children with their schoolwork. Mom decided the kids were really capable of doing their own schoolwork. One of the children threw a fit about this, telling Mom it was her job to help him do it and he wouldn't do well if she didn't help. She held firm by telling him that she knew he really could handle the work and that she'd written a note to his teacher asking for her help if he had any problems. In doing this she avoided falling into the "pity trap" he'd tried to set for her.

9. BE CREATIVE IN ADDING NEW WORK EXPERIENCES.

Sometimes we underestimate what our kids can do and overestimate what we "should" do. As the kids get older, they may want to take over all the laundry or do the grocery shopping alone. What's important is not whether a task is divided evenly, but that everyone in the family has opportunities to make a contribution. If you're open to that way of thinking, you may decide to swap the dinner dishes that the kids have been doing for some of the cooking that you've handled. The possibilities are limitless, and the faith in your kids can go a long way in building maturity.

10. ENCOURAGE WORK OUTSIDE THE HOME.

Another way to help children feel good about themselves is to encourage them to seek work outside the home. At this age they can babysit for neighbors' children, house-sit, wash cars, do yardwork, handle paper routes, do housecleaning, work in local stores or restaurants, or hire out for clean-up projects or construction jobs. In one family the parents were able to hire their son to do filing and typing at their office. The boy felt important and capable and was also able to provide extra income to cover some of his personal expenses. The family took this opportunity to sit down, reevaluate their plan for doing Family Work, and make some adjustments.

11. FOCUS ON KEEPING AGREEMENTS AND THE MEANING OF FAMILY.

Kids in this age group can understand things in different ways. When they were younger a logical consequence or making a game out of cleanup might have worked. Now they can understand that keeping agreements is part of trust, which is the basis of a strong relationship. Kids this age need to hear and understand that what they do affects their relationships with others and that if they want to be trusted, they have a share in that by keeping agreements.

Kids can also understand that part of being in a family is respecting each other and not taking relationships for granted. A family functions best when everyone pulls together. At this age kids can influence what kind of family they would like to have by their own actions.

But part of being in a family is knowing that we don't have to be perfect. We can trust each other and remember that we all have the best interests of the family and each other at stake even when we may be slacking off or having a bad day, or even a bad month. This faith in each other can go a long way toward helping each other and getting over the rough spots.

CHAPTER 6 - QUESTIONS YOU MAY HAVE ASKED
YOURSELF

1. What if a family member doesn't want to pick a job?

It may take a little time and training to get a reluctant family member to cooperate. If someone in your family is unwilling to pick a job, you can give her or him several choices: (1) participate willingly; (2) accept jobs assigned by the other family members; or (3) take what's left after everyone else has chosen. Make it clear that not selecting a job isn't one of the choices. Another approach would be to appeal to the family member's sense of good will or fair play--"Does it seem fair to you that someone shouldn't have to do his or her share along with the rest of the family?" You might also communicate that you really NEED and APPRECIATE the help. You could then negotiate to see what he or she would be willing to do that would be helpful. Accept an initial offer and be willing to work toward more participation in the future. This avoids the possibility of getting into a power struggle over the issue of "it's got to be done my way" or "it's not enough." Remember, you're working toward progress, not perfection!

Another approach is to offer to work with the family member. This is good for older kids who may never have learned how to do something but find it embarrassing to say so. This way you can teach as you work together.

You also might decide to leave certain jobs undone and allow the family to experience the results. You could meet together the following week and discuss how each person feels about what happened and what needs to be done about it. Some families have a discussion about what it means to participate in the family. They discuss questions such as: If you don't want to work, does that mean you don't want to participate in the family and what does that mean? Any understandings you arrive at must be clear to and agreed upon by all family members. Attitudes are extremely important here. The point is not just to get kids to do things your way. That will only lead to resistance and rebellion--not cooperation.

2. What do you do if a person is signed up for a job and isn't there?

Consider whether or not this job can wait until the person returns. Vacuuming and lawn mowing are examples of jobs that can wait. But some jobs can't wait. The table has to be set before each meal, for example. This can be handled in several ways. The person whose job it is can do the job before leaving. She or he can make arrangements in advance with another family member to fill in. Before the son in one family left for summer camp he obtained the agreement of the other members of the family to care for his guinea pig. Sometimes family members are willing to do jobs for pay, and this too can be negotiated in advance. Some families include the position of "alternate" in their job planning. This person then fills in and does the jobs when other family members are absent. This could be set up during the regular job planning process.

3. What happens if the job doesn't get done?

It would be nice if everything ran smoothly as planned, but often that's not the case. On these occasions you might feel discouraged and think about giving up. But that won't take care of the problem. When breakdowns occur in Family Work, it's important for the family to sit down and discuss what needs to be done. Stick with it and work out solutions that everyone can live with. But don't give up.

4. Should we pay kids to do jobs?

The danger in paying kids for doing jobs is that they learn to do work only when they get something for it. Will they pick up their socks if they get only five cents a sock? We believe that children should receive an allowance because they're part of the family and are entitled to a share of the family's "wealth." Being a member of the family also means there's Family Work to be done, and the family members need to cooperate on this. There are also some "extra" jobs you might be willing to pay someone to do. You can make a list of these so your kids have the opportunity to earn extra money if they wish.

5. What if the family refuses to work?

This doesn't happen too often, but in some families members are not willing to make changes, especially if they've been used to special service for a long time. If appealing to your family's sense of fairness doesn't get their cooperation, you can take stronger measures.

In some cases parental "strike" can do the trick. This is a powerful strategy, though, and it should be used as a last resort after you've tried the other suggestions from this book. A strike is based on the assumption that you have the right to want family involvement in Family Work. You may not be able to make the family comply, but you can decide what you will or will not do. A strike means you take care of your own needs--prepare food for yourself, make your bed, clean your clothes, and so on--but you refuse to take care of other family members' needs.

If you take this somewhat drastic step, you should be prepared for the disorganization and chaos that will ensue.

It's important to let family members know what you're doing and then follow through while maintaining an attitude of friendliness--to be both firm and kind. Don't cave in when your fifteen-year-old pleads that she has nothing clean to wear to the dance and her life will be ruined. You can reply in a sincere and friendly tone that you're sorry and you know how hard it must be for her. After experiencing the discomfort of the chaos for a few days, most families are willing to come together and discuss the changes that need to take place. Then you can begin the process with the suggestions on page 30. Take heart. One family felt the effects of a parental strike for six weeks before they were willing to cooperate.

6. What if I have nothing to do?

It's really okay to enjoy the extra time. You can put your feet up, read a book, go for a walk, take a leisurely bath, watch a TV show, talk to a friend, smell the flowers--anything you like to do for you; the list is endless. You don't have to be busy and doing something all the time. If you find yourself with extra time, it doesn't have to be spent playing with the kids. It's okay to take care of and be good to YOU!

7. What happens if we slip?

It helps if you can look at a slip as just that--a slip. It doesn't have to be a DISASTER. You need to have the family members sit down and talk about what's happened and find out why the others think things aren't working. Then start again.

8. What happens if I keep picking the same job or don't like the job I have?

This is a time when you can ask the family for help. Bring this problem up at one of your family meetings. Other family members can be a great resource for new ideas. Don't be afraid to try it. If you've been picking jobs from a hat, you might try rotating jobs for a while or even trade jobs. Be willing to change your system if it's not working. It helps to set up a time to evaluate how the system is working. This can keep you from becoming locked into something your family doesn't like after they've done it for a while.

9. How long will it take to get my family to do Family Work together?

It helps to think in terms of not having a "finish line." Dealing with Family Work is a continually and evolving process. Sometimes the training may seem as if it is taking forever while at other times change occurs quickly. Changing old patterns usually takes time. It's easy to want things to change all at once, but this won't happen. It can be discouraging, and you may feel like giving up. Focus on the progress that your family has made. Ask each family member to take a few minutes and assess how far you've all come. Notice the little successes. Build on these small successes, and they'll develop into big accomplishments over time.

10. Will they still need a Mom if I don't do it all?

Absolutely! In fact they'll need you more, but in different ways. As the parent you'll now be thinking ahead and helping your family learn to plan. You'll be guiding and teaching your children to develop new skills--skills that will help them be better equipped to handle the demands life will make of them. You will be teaching them to focus on what needs to be done and how they can help. You'll probably find there's still plenty to do. If you do have a great deal of extra time, you can volunteer your services in the community, take a class, or host an exchange student.

11. Where do I start?

The best place to start is changing your attitude from thinking you have to be responsible for doing it all to "work is the job of the whole family." Once you've done that you need to approach your family in the ways suggested in chapters 1 and 2. It's also important to start with something in which the family can experience some success, to pick something small at first. Involve all family members, including the youngest child. It's easy to feel that little ones aren't ready or old enough yet, but it's important that they learn to feel capable and part of the family.

12. Once we start this, do we have to do it forever?

Everyone likes a break--a vacation from work now and then. There's no reason why this can't happen with Family Work. One caution is that the family members should agree on how and when this will occur. Some suggestions that may come up are (1) to throw out your charts for a certain amount of time, (2) to allow each family member to take a "vacation" from work for a week or so, or (3) if you're using a chart, add a slot for a free week. In one family the person who was free also served as an alternate, filing in for whoever wasn't there to do his or her job.

13. What about doing jobs as gifts?

The could be a good way of showing that you feel appreciative or good about another family member. One family found how nice it was to surprise someone by doing that person's job for them. In another family one of the kids made a coupon book for his mother for Mother's Day. She could "cash in" the coupons at any time in exchange for his doing several of her jobs. This could also work well for birthdays, anniversaries, or any days.

14. How do I respond to statements like, "You're home all day, why can't you do the housework?" and "Does this mean I'm supposed to work at the office all day and come and do YOUR work too?"

This question comes up frequently, especially in families that have been rather traditional in determining the division of labor. Unfortunately, "housework" often winds up being a 24-hour-a-day, seven-day-a-week job that can lead to a lot of built-up resentments. One approach is to have a family meeting to discuss exactly what "housework" means. List all the jobs--for example, those that need to be done daily, weekly, or at certain times during the week. Include jobs like scheduling appointments, driving to soccer practice or dancing lessons, baking cookies for school, taking care of the cars, yardwork, preparing snacks, and washing cars. These are often forgotten or taken for granted, but they count as work. When there's a clear understanding of all the things that have to be done, family members will be better prepared to decide who will do what and when. Thus, Family Work can be negotiated and jobs divided so it will work for your family. This doesn't mean that everything will be divided equally, but it does mean that the work is divided by agreement and not by assumption.

Some families may not reach complete agreement. That's okay. You can decide what you will do--change can start with your doing things differently. This is especially helpful in families where the woman works outside the home and also feels responsible for doing all "her" housework.

15. Is the point of all this so you can have a spotlessly clean "Good Housekeeping" type of house?

No. A clean, orderly house is a side benefit of Family Work. The main benefit is that Family Work provides an opportunity for all family members to feel useful and have a sense of belonging. Through Family Work parents teach their children new skills and develop a spirit of cooperation in the family. They foster an attitude of "We're all in this together and we can make it work." Children learn to focus on the needs of the situation and ask, "What can I do to help?" A feeling of closeness and true concern for others develops.

ABOUT THE AUTHORS

Lynn Lott, M.A., M.F.C.C., is the founder and executive director of the Family Education Center in Petaluma, California. In addition to her private practice as a counselor, she conducts workshops for parents, couples, teachers, counselors and businesses. She also teaches at Sonoma State University.

Lynn is co-author of *To Know Me Is To Love Me; Changing Your Relationship with Your Teen;* and *Married and Liking It.*

Married and the mother of two teens, Lynn lives in Santa Rosa, California.

Riki Intner, M.A., M.F.C.C., has extensive experience counseling families, couples and individuals. Much of her time in recent years has been devoted to working with families of chemically dependent people. Riki is past chairperson of the board of directors of The Family Education Center.

Married and the mother of three teens, Riki also lives in Santa Rosa, California.

Marilyn Kientz is a parent educator for The Family Education Center and administrator for a foreign exchange student program, Cultural Homestay Institute. Marilyn is also a drama instructor for elementary school students. She is co-author of *To Know Me Is To Love Me.*

Married and the mother of two teens and one toddler, Marilyn lives in Petaluma, California.

Additional copies of this book can be ordered from:

The Practical Press
P.O. Box 2615
Petaluma, California 94953

BOOKS BY THE PRACTICAL PRESS:

Changing Your Relationship With Your Teen
  by Lynn Lott and Dru West $4.00
Family Work: Whose Job Is It?
by Lynn Lott, Riki Intner & Marilyn Kentz $9.95
Married and Liking It
  by Lynn Lott-Penny and Dru West $7.95
To Know Me Is To Love Me
by Lynn Lott-Penny, Marilyn Kentz
and Dru West $10.00
Teaching Parenting
by Lynn Lott with Jane Allen   manual with 2 texts
                                             $50.00
                                 manual only
                                             $40.00

Four Sets of Overhead Transfers for making Transparencies
For use in seminars, parenting classes, and therapy
Set A: Positive Parenting & Teaching
Set B: Teens
Set C: Chemical Dependency
Set D: Healing the Whole Person

                                     $10.00 per set or
                                     $25.00 all four

California residents add 6% sales tax
Shipping $1.40 for 1st item & $.40 for each additional item

Prices effective September 1989 and are subject to change
without notice.